lib. Skills - TOP Dewey

The <u>most</u> <u>excellent</u> book of
how to be a
cheerleader

Bob Kiralfy

Illustrated by Rob Shone and Peter Harper

Stargazer Books

New edition 2007

© Aladdin Books Ltd
1997
Designed and produced by
Aladdin Books Ltd

*New edition published in
the United States in 2007
by Stargazer Books*
c/o The Creative
Company
123 South Broad Street
P.O. Box 227
Mankato, Minnesota
56002

Illustrators
Rob Shone
Peter Harper

Printed in
the United States

**Library of Congress
Cataloging-in-Publication Data**

Kiralfy, Bob.
  How to be a cheerleader / by
Bob Kiralfy.
    p. cm. -- (Most excellent
book of--)
  Previous ed: Most excellent book
of how to be a cheerleader. 1997.
  ISBN 978-1-59604-128-8
  1. Cheerleading--Juvenile
literature. I. Kiralfy, Bob. Most
excellent book of how to be a
cheerleader. II. Title. III. Series.

LB3635.K57 2007
791.6'4--dc22
                2005057623

CONTENTS

INTRODUCTION

Cheerleading is almost 100 years old. The first cheerleaders were led by Johnny Campbell at a University of Minnesota football game in 1898. Realizing that his team needed some encouragement, Johnny led the crowd with some cheers – to great effect.

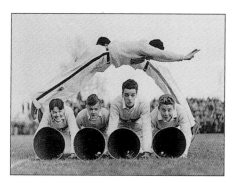

Originally, all cheerleaders were men *(left)*; it was only in the 1920s that women *(above)* became actively involved in cheerleading. Today, millions of cheerleaders, in countries around the world, cheer for different sports from car racing to swimming.

Would you like to be out on the sidelines, leading cheers for your team? You can! Read on to find out how you can become a cheerleader. Have fun!

As you read the book, look for these symbols:
★ *tells you what you will need to make your cheerleading accessories and gives you tips on cheerleading techniques.*
✔ *gives you hints on how to perfect your performance.*

Leading CHEERS

The louder the better! Encourage your team to win with the best and loudest cheers.

At many sports events you will often see cheerleaders, in brightly colored uniforms – and with even brighter smiles – supporting the competing teams.

Cheerleaders perform before the game and at halftime, as well as leading chants during the game for their teams. Some sports have short breaks during the game called "time-outs." This is when the cheerleaders keep the atmosphere going with dances and cheers.

Enthusiastic cheers and chants can make the difference between winning and losing for your team.

Cheerleaders can start from five years old as "Peewees." Most cheerleaders are of school age, cheering for the love of it (above).

There are times to cheer...

1 When your team is on the field or court;

2 When player substitutions are being made;

3 When exceptionally good plays are made;

4 When your team scores;

5 As a tribute to injured players, once they get up and head for the sidelines;

6 As encouragement throughout the game;

7 During time-outs and halftime.

... and there are times not to cheer

1 When referee signals are being made;

2 When any player is injured;

3 When official announcements are being made;

4 After time-outs and other intervals when the referee signals the game to restart.

★ *Always be positive. Never encourage the audience to taunt the other team or to criticize the referees. As a cheerleader, you are a model of good sporting behavior.*

A *cheerful* UNIFORM

Design a uniform to match your team or school colors.

Pom-poms can be made from paper (see page 8), in colors to match your uniform.

★ *To make your cheerleading uniform, you will need: a sports skirt; a sweater or sweatshirt; a sleeveless top or T-shirt; white socks and white sneakers; a piece of felt; fabric paint or glitter; braiding; glue; a tape measure, scissors, a needle, and thread.*

Wear white socks and comfortable white sneakers.

Tie your hair back neatly to prevent it from falling in your eyes when you start jumping around!

Be prepared for any weather! Wear a colorful sweater or a sweatshirt with a sleeveless top, or a T-shirt.

Wear a pleated skirt of regular athletic length.

✔ *Avoid wearing jewelry when you are in your cheerleading uniform... but do wear a smile!*

You don't have to buy special clothes – use your imagination to create your own eye-catching uniform from items of clothing you may already have.

Designing your top

To add your team's initials to your uniform, draw the letters on a piece of felt. Cut out *(above)* and sew them onto your sweatshirt, sleeveless top, or T-shirt. Stick glitter or paint a team emblem onto a piece of felt. Cut out the emblem and sew it onto your top.

Designing your skirt

The box-pleated skirt, with pleats of contrasting colors *(above)*, is the traditional style of a cheerleader's skirt. The knife-pleated skirt, to which you can add braiding *(above right)*, is also popular. Measure around the bottom of your skirt with a tape measure. Buy a length of braiding *(left)* from a department store. Sew it around your skirt, about an inch (2.5cm) above the bottom edge.

Cheerful pom-POMS

Make your own colorful pom-poms

★ *You will need: several sheets of colored paper – choose colors to complement your uniform; scissors; glue or masking tape; two pieces of plain cardboard, or two paper towel tubes.*

1 Make parallel cuts in the sheets of contrasting colored paper .5 in (13mm) apart. Leave approximately 1 in (2.5cm) uncut at one end.

2 Stack the paper sheets on top of each other.

3 Tape or glue one piece of cardboard into a thin tube shape. Place this (or the empty paper towel tube) on top of the paper sheets.

4 Roll the paper sheets tightly around the tube. Glue or tape them together at their uncut end.

5 Fold back the paper strands so that you can cut the tube, leaving only a short handle at the end with the uncut paper.

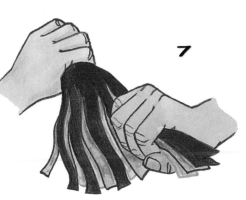

6 Repeat to make your second pom-pom.

7 Until you fluff them up, your pom-poms will look flat and uninteresting. Scrunch each strand (cut piece of paper) between your fingers, to shape each one into a ball.

Using your pom-poms

The main purpose of pom-poms ("poms" for short) is to make your arm movements *(see page 12)* stand out, so that everyone can see you – even the crowds at the back of the stands in a big stadium.

Hold your poms so that the strands almost cover your hands. Your starting position is with your feet apart and your hands on your hips. With or without poms, this is also the best position to hold at games when you are not actually cheering.

✔ *Using poms requires big, precise movements. Hold each move for an instant before moving sharply onto the next.*

Warming UP

Before practice or performance it is important to "warm up."

Why warm up?
Cheerleading involves a lot of physical activity. To prevent injury, warm up before every training session and every game. A warm-up period should last for at least 20 minutes. These pages show you just a few exercises to include in your warm-up. Why not ask a gym teacher at school to suggest some others?

3

1 Give your wrists a good stretch by interlocking your fingers. Bend at both wrists, slowly moving one hand above the other.

2 Stretch each arm up, down, and around. As you do so, you should feel a stretch along your sides.

3 Slowly rotate or turn your head in a big circle. Move it slowly from side to side and then from back to front.

4 Begin with some slow running in place. Gradually increase your speed.

5 Circle your ankles first in one direction and then in the other. Point and flex your feet.

6 Interlock your fingers; press your arms out in front of you, turning your palms away from you. This will stretch your upper back.

7 Move both your shoulders up and down, and around in circles, backward and forward. Raise one shoulder several times, and then the other.

★ *Always stretch slowly and never force a stretch.*

Move those ARMS!

Arm motions are the essential movements for cheers, chants, and sharp dance routines.

High "V"

Daggers

Clasp

Diagonal

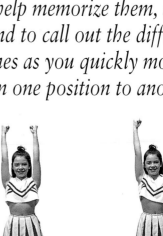

★ *Practice the motions in front of a mirror. Stand up straight with your feet apart. To help memorize them, ask a friend to call out the different names as you quickly move from one position to another.*

Low "V"

"T"

Vertical

Touchdown

Punch-up

Loud and CLEAR

"Defense, Attack, Get That Ball Back!"

Carrying your voice

Most cheerleading squads do not have a big stadium sound system; they have to use their voices *(below)*. To make your voice carry, take deep breaths; use your stomach muscles to help power the words – don't just use your throat. Form each sound clearly. Sounds that flow into each other cannot carry over a distance, especially if there is a large group shouting together.

De • FenSe
A • TtacK *(pause)*
Get • That • Ball
• BacK!

Cheers and chants have a special rhythm and timing. This is to make sure that everybody can hear you clearly. A typical chant *(above)* can be broken down into clear single sounds, as shown. Emphasize the letters in capitals.

Making a MEGAPHONE

A megaphone amplifies or increases sound – so everyone can hear you.

★ *You will need: a sheet of thick cardboard 27.5 x 27.5 inches (70x70cm) or a thin plastic sheet; a ruler; a pencil; scissors; glue, masking tape or paper fasteners; and paint.*

1 Draw the megaphone shape on the cardboard in pencil.

2 From the remaining cardboard, cut a strip about 4 inches (10cm) wide and 12 inches (30cm) long. This will become your handle.

3 Paint the cone in your team colors. Paint on a team emblem or make one out of felt and glue it on. Add your team's initial letter.

4 Glue, tape, or use paper fasteners to attach these edges together.

5 Curve the megaphone shape into a cone, overlapping the straight edges.

23.5 in (60cm)

6 in (15cm)

23.5 in (60cm)

6 Roll the length of cardboard (step 2) into a tight cone. Tape or glue it together.

7 At each end of the cone make parallel cuts at 0.5-in (13-mm) intervals. Each cut should be about 1 in (2.5cm) in length.

8 Bend these outward to form small flaps.

9 Curve the cone into a handle shape. Glue or tape the flaps of the handle to the megaphone. Use paper fasteners to attach the handle to the megaphone.

★ *When you use your megaphone to amplify your voice (below), hold the narrow end with one hand and the handle with the other hand. Hold it at a slightly raised angle.*

✔ *With a little practice and creativity, you will be able to use your megaphone to add to your cheering skills. Use it as a visual prop. Bring it sharply down to your side between each word or line of the chant or cheer. Swing it diagonally upward from your knee to a high "V" in time with the music. Use it like a drum, banging the side of it with the palm of your hand (above).*

Flash those CARDS!

Flash cards help you to prompt the crowd response during a game.

★ *You will need: several sheets of stiff cardboard, approximately 29 inches x 16 inches (74cm x 41cm) – choose a variety of colors; a pencil; poster paints; glue; and clear plastic wrap.*

I Select words that you can mix and match to form chants – for example, "Eagles," "Go," "Win," "Blue," and "White." Have different words or phrases on each card.

2 Glue two different colored sheets of cardboard together.

3 In pencil, outline the word or phrase on the card. Use words or phrases that follow each other on opposite sides of the card – for example, "Go" on one side and "Eagles" on the other – with "Eagles" upside down.

4 Cover the cards with clear plastic wrap to make them last longer.

Using your flash cards

1 At a key point in the game, when a chant would really liven things up, pick up your flash card by its short edges. Hold it out in front of you so the audience can't see what's on the card.

2 If your chant is "Go, Eagles, Go," as you chant "Go," hold up the card showing the word "Go."

3 When you chant "Eagles," turn the card in your hands so "Eagles" is visible. When you chant "Go," turn the card back again.

★ *With some cheerleading friends and several flash cards, you can spell out whole cheers (see pages 24-26) to prompt the audience to chant back.*

✔ *Don't let the audience see the word or phrase on the card until the moment you shout it out. For effect, hold it out in front of you for an instant – then turn it quickly to face the audience. Hold the card above your head, so the audience can see your face.*

Chant for your TEAM

Chants are short routines that you repeat to involve the crowd during a game. Try with "Let's Go Bulldogs, Let's Go!"

"Let's"   "Go"   "Bull"

1   2   3

Begin with your left foot pointed and your weight on your right foot. Swap for each move.

1 Put your left hand on your left hip and your right hand on your right shoulder.

2 Sharply punch your right arm up and slightly forward.

3 Bring both arms to the front, with your elbows to the sides.

"Dogs"

5 Bring your right hand to your hip with your elbow out to your side. Take your left hand to your left shoulder with your elbow forward.

"Let's"

4 Take your arms out to a "T" motion.

"Go"

7 Clap your pom-poms together twice in front of you to create a pause in the chant. Repeat the chant from the start.

6 Punch your left arm up, and slightly forward.

Keep transferring your weight from one foot to the other.

★ *Use your own team name instead of "Bulldogs."*

More *cheerful* CHANTING

"Go white, out of sight! Go red, win tonight!"

"Go"

"White"

"Out"

✔ Make your arm motions sharp and clear. Practice them in time with your chant.

1

2

3

In this chant stand with your feet apart.

"Of"

"Sight"

✔ Use your own team colors instead of "white" and "red."

4

5

I Begin with a clasp.

2 Punch into a high "V."

3 Punch into a vertical.

4 Move to a crossed "V."

5 Lower the "V."

6 Clasp your hands together. **7** Punch into a high "V." **8** Punch into a vertical.

"Go"   "Red"

6

7

"Win"

8

"To"

"Night"

9 Move to a crossed "V."
10 Move your arms to a high "V."

9

10

✔ *Keep your chants simple and easy to join in with. Clap or bang out a rhythm on megaphones or drums to encourage people to clap and wave back. Keep eye contact with the audience.*

Jumping JACKS!

Add some jumps and leaps into your cheers and dances.

★ *Always warm up properly* (see pages 10-11) *before you practice your jumps and wear the correct footwear. Begin with some small hops. Then try small jumps such as the tuck* (see opposite page).

Toe-touch jump

1 Stand up straight with your arms in a high "V."
2 Swing your arms downward, slightly bending at the knees.
3 Use your arms and shoulders to give you a good "lift-off." Explode upward, kicking up with your toes. Bring your toes to your hands.

3

2

4 Land lightly on the balls of your feet... and smile!

★ *Practice on a mat, with plenty of space around you! Bend your knees when you land.*

Tuck jump

1 Swing your arms down to create energy to jump.

2 Jump straight up into the air, bringing your knees into your chest. Keep your knees as close together as possible and try to point your toes.

3 Land gently on the balls of your feet.

✔ *Your team has just done something spectacular. Get the audience fired up with an explosion of energy!*

Stag jump

1 Stand up straight with your arms in a high "V."

2 Swing your arms down and up in a strong circular motion.

3 Spring up as your arms circle upward. Bend one leg underneath as the other extends behind you.

4 Land gently on the balls of your feet.

CHEERS!

Cheers are longer routines performed at intervals or time-outs.

1 Begin in the starting position *(see page 9)*.

Each word of the cheer is accompanied by a numbered move 1-13 (see page 26).

2 Bend your knees. Bring your arms together.

3 Take your arms to a low "V."

4 Stand tall and punch your arms into a touchdown.

5 Bend your right leg and arm; put your left hand on your hip.

6 Cross your right arm over your body. Your legs don't move.

7 Straighten your leg and punch your arms to a high "V."

Bull **(1)** dogs **(2)** • fans **(3)** • up **(4)** • in **(5)** • the **(6)** • stands **(7)** •
Are **(1)** • you **(2)** • ready **(3)** • to **(4)** • yell **(5)** • and **(6)** • cheer **(7)**? •
This **(11)** • side **(12)** • yell **(13)** • "Go" **(7)** • – *Go!* **(4)** •
This **(12)** • side **(13)** • yell **(2)** • "Red" **(3)** • – *Red!* **(7)** •
Bull **(1)** dogs **(2)** • fans **(3)** • gonna **(4)** • party **(5)** • to **(6)** night **(7)** •
Yelling **(2)** • "Go" **(3)** • "Red" **(7)** • "Go" **(3)** • "Red" **(7)** •

11   **12**   **13**

8 Bend your right leg and arm; put your left hand on your hip.
9 Turn your body and legs to the left.
10 Bend your knees; move your arms to a vertical motion.
11 Move into a low "V."
12 & 13 Follow steps 5 and 6, but use opposite arms and legs.

Chant each word of the cheer (*above*) to the move numbered.

Parade TIME

Parades and carnivals are a lot of fun. Cheerleaders perform on the move with marching bands and decorated floats.

From the United States to the United Kingdom, cheerleaders add excitement and color to a parade or carnival *(right* and *below)*, encouraging the crowd to wave and cheer back. Big crowds line the streets. Most cheers and chants can be adapted for parades by simply using the arm motions and words while marching.

★ *If the parade is moving slowly, add leg and body movements, and even dance, so long as each step carries you forward. You can also use big flags or banners.*

✔ *When you are performing in a parade, you need to have continuous movement and plenty of energy. You are only in front of each section of the crowd for a short time so give each section a special show.*

Dancing DAYS

Dance routines are an excellent way to entertain a crowd.

★ *Depending on the game you are supporting, you will have approximately 45-60 seconds during a time-out for your dance routine. Routines are usually based on 8 or 16 beats – choose music that has a regular beat, such as funk or hip-hop.*

1 Step forward with your right leg.

✔ Give your moves a lot of energy.

2 Raise your right leg. Punch your right arm up.

3 Punch your arms out to a "T." Turn your feet to the left.

4 Turn to the front. Step back with your left leg. Bring your elbows in.

5 Punch your right arm up. Move your left arm back.

6 Bend at your knees. Stretch your right arm out.

7 Punch forward and kick back with your right leg.

8 Kick up with your right leg. Punch down with your hands.

✔ *With some friends, make up your own dance routine.*

Competition TIME

Many countries have cheerleading competitions. The largest is in Nashville, Tennessee, where over 200 squads compete.

In national and international competitions each squad performs a three-minute routine that includes cheers, chants, jumps, dance, tumbling, and building pyramids. Music can only be used for half of the routine. Pom-poms, flash cards, and megaphones are used in competitions as well as at games.

You may sometimes see cheerleaders at games performing pyramids. Do not try this without special training – the cheerleaders *(left)* have been specially trained.

✔ *Build your own routine by combining cheers, chants, and dance. Make it into one continuous routine without pauses. Add some jumps.*

Game DAY

Game day at last! This is where you can have the best time, supporting your team, and helping the crowd have fun.

Cheerleaders usually perform a routine before the game starts called "pre-game." They then form two lines as a "tunnel" for the players to run through as they are announced to the crowd *(below)*. This is a great opportunity to use jumps and high kicks to encourage loud applause.

When play is in motion, use simple one and two-word chants to get the best response. At halftime a special, longer routine is performed. Work out a winning combination of dance, cheers, and chants.

★ *Show tact and good sporting behavior if your team is ahead. Give extra energy and encouragement if your team is behind.*

Cheerful WORDS

Chants Short routines with words.

Cheers Longer routines with words.

Defense When the other team has the ball.

Flash cards Cards that show the crowd which words to shout back.

Megaphone A cone to amplify your voice.

Offense When your team has the ball.

Routine A sequence of moves.

Scrunching Fluffing up pom-poms into a ball shape.

Time-outs Short intervals in a game.

INDEX

Keep on CHEERING!

Make up your own chants, cheers, and routines. With a group of friends, ask your school if you can start a cheerleading squad to cheer for its sports teams.

Picture credits
Abbreviations: t-top, m-middle, b-bottom, r-right, l-left
All photography by Roger Vlitos except for: cover br, 13, 27 both, 30b – Bob Kiralfy; 3b, 4r, & 31 – Mark Sandom; 3t & m – Archive Photos; cover tl – John Marsden.